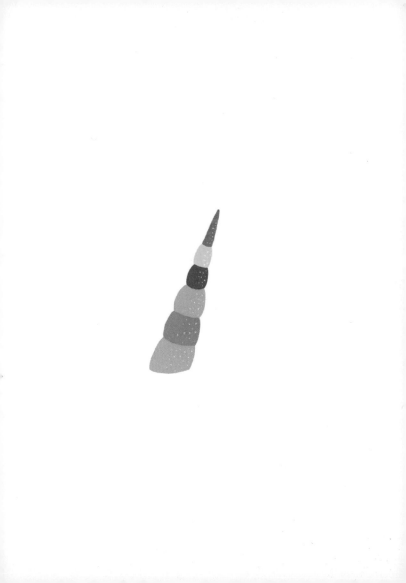

BE MORE UNICORN

HOW TO FIND YOUR INNER SPARKLE

Words by Joanna Gray

Illustrations by Carolyn Suzuki

quadrille

BE MORE...

FOREWORD

We were two small girls who played beneath the boughs of a lilac bush. My cousin and I were close. We made perfume from rose petals, stood back-to-back as we sang, and invented a fantasy world we returned to summer after summer.

In the garden of our grandparents' cottage we made our fairy queen palace. The lilac bush grew wild at the end of the lawn. The floor was packed earth and the branches sufficiently low-hanging to turn into shelves. We hung tin mugs from twigs and brought our picnics to eat cross-legged in our palace.

One summer afternoon, when the light was beginning to fade, we decided we wanted more. We decided being fairy queens in our very own lilac palace wasn't enough. We wanted a companion. We wanted something to look after. We wanted something to further extend our adventure in our very own paradise. We whispered the deepest desires of little girls: a kitten, a goose that would lay sugared eggs,

Rapunzel. It was my cousin who conjured the unicorn. I can still hear her whisper now. The very word was magical: "unicorn" rustled between the blossoms.

It took only a look, an agreement between us, for everything to shift that one summer twilight evening. We simply stood up, held hands and closed our eyes. Saying "unicorn" together was all it took. We opened our eyes and saw it standing, quivering in the corner. The unicorn was small, perhaps the size of a large dog. Blossoms hung down but its pearlescent horn almost reached the ceiling of our fairy–tale bower. So white was its coat that we both raised our hands to our eyes. We crouched down and edged towards this most beautiful of creatures. Wonder had filled the lilac bush, time shook and we were sure we had unlocked a world of deep country magic. What happened next, remains secret, between me, my cousin and our unicorn.

I am now a grown woman with three children of my own. I no longer make fairy palaces, nor pretend to be a pop star. However my cousin and I are still close and cling to our idyllic childhood, where our imaginations were free to roam.

I also continue to conjure unicorns.

As an adult mired in the world of hard work, of domestic drudgery, of city commuting, it is vital to be able to access again the spirit of childhood magic. So I continue to conjure the unicorn.

When I cannot see beauty around me, I summon the unicorn. When I feel I cannot achieve something, I summon the unicorn. When I feel alone and without support, I summon the unicorn. Its beauty, innocence and awesome qualities help me to focus and reset.

I hope this small book brings the magical inspiration of the unicorn to you, too. Close your eyes and enter into the mythical world of unicorns. Let them walk beside you, through life's challenges. Let their grace and glory teach you how to *Be More Unicorn*.

Joanna Gray

INTRODUCTION

You could be forgiven for thinking that unicorns galloped onto the scene the day before yesterday. Whether it's cupcakes, coffee or crayons, unicorns have got them covered in glitter, sparkles and rainbows. However, this isn't a marketing fad. Unicorns have seized the human imagination for millennia.

The current lust for all things unicorn is nothing new – in medieval times unicorns inspired a similar frenzy, with fashionable folk vying for the lastest unicorn tapestry, while popes and monarchs in the Tudor period spent the equivalent of millions of pounds buying unicorn horns. Quack doctors in the 18th century peddled ground-up unicorn horns as a cure-all for sickness bugs, and Victorian explorers set off to discover real live unicorns in the field.

Unicorn hysteria is as old as time. Greek physician, Ctesias of Cnidus first wrote about unicorns frolicking in India in the 5th century BC.

He's not the only sage to be entranced by the exquisite horned horse. Luminaries such as Aristotle, Julius Caesar and Leonardo da Vinci have all written about unicorns, investigating their habitat, physique and temperament.

Rationalists and pedants might insist that these great men were actually witnessing the rhinoceros or the ibex, and that the unicorn as a living beast could not possibly exist. While we, of course, say *bah humbug* to them, there is no doubt that the unicorn, as a firm figment of the human imagination, certainly does exist.

Its existence in myth, legend and folklore has inspired the highest of arts. What other legendary creature can be found in Renaissance paintings, Shakespeare's plays and on the Royal Coat of Arms of the United Kingdom?

While its form has changed throughout the ages, morphing in size from a neat lapdog to a bulbous elephant, the core qualities of a unicorn have remained constant.

Chronicles tell such beguiling stories of the unicorn purifying water, fighting with their horn to defend their young and lying in the laps of young women. This shows that the unicorn is a uniquely gentle creature that has power, but chooses to use it for good alone.

In revelling in the cultural history of the unicorn it becomes clear that ten attributes of the unicorn emerge time and time again. This small book, the latest in a long history of love letters to the unicorn, offers these unicorn characteristics for readers to play with. Unicorns are magical, fabulous, enigmatic, powerful, graceful, chimeric, playful, fierce, innocent and fulfilling. In understanding these glorious aspects of the unicorn and applying them to daily life, we hope you may find a way to *Be More Unicorn*.

Liberal amounts of glitter and sparkle are also required!

BE MORE...
MAGICAL

LET
unicorn
magic
CAST
ITS SPELL

UNICORNS ARE...
MAGICAL

ˈmædʒɪkl: beautiful or delightful in a way that seems removed from everyday life

"Those who don't believe in magic never find it," holds true to the world of unicorns. You have to believe in the magic of unicorns in order to fully appreciate their glory. Once you've suspended reason, the magical world of unicorns is open to all who seek it.

Before you read this chapter, please close your eyes and keep them closed. Wait for two minutes and listen to what's happening around you. Feel the touch of your skin, breathe deeply and wait for the magic of the unicorn to descend.

Try it now. Close your eyes. Picture the unicorn – its glimmering horn, its rippling flanks, its perfectly curled lashes and its beauty.

Now slowly open your eyes and whisper:

"I believe in unicorns"

To conjure the spirit of the unicorn is to enter the realm of true make-believe. It is to step into our own childhoods and to be charmed by the exquisite.

"I believe in unicorns"

Magic is believing in yourself. If you can do that, you can make anything happen.

Johann Goethe

Magic and unicorns have played with each other since the deepest past. There is one story about the unicorn's benign use of magic that has travelled with the blessed creature through the ages...

It's dawn; the forest is stirring awake. The mice are scurrying for nuts, the deer are breathing the dew-damp air and the birds are singing to herald the sun.

Little do they realize that at nightfall, the serpent slithered to the lake with evil intent, and with one flick of its tongue, it poisoned the watering hole.

Yet at dawn, the unicorn appears on the shore, as fleeting as quicksilver. Its bright white flanks gleam against the woodland glade. It dips its head and the horn touches the water. A magical jolt of energy darts from the horn and in an instant the water is cleansed of the serpent's poison. As sun breaks out from the morning mist, the animals safely drink the purified water.

With a flick of her tail and mane, the unicorn disappears. She leaves only a brief whisper of magical kindness.

With such power the unicorn could use this magic to assert authority over the other creatures. But good nature means the unicorn is happy to share her magical skill for no benefit to herself at all.

For centuries unicorns' horns were used in medicine to protect against food poisoning. Alicon, as it was known, was sold by apothecaries in London until the 18th century.

"To this day it is said, that malicious animals poison this water after sundown, so that none can there upon drink it. But early in the morning, as soon as the sun rises, a unicorn comes out of the ocean, dips his horn into the water to expel the venom from it, so that other animals may drink thereof during the day. This as I describe it, I have seen with my own eyes." Johannes Von Hesse, Utrecht, 1389

The magic that the unicorn emanates is entirely beneficial. It's a soothing, healing, protective magic. To be as magical as the unicorn doesn't require supernatural powers. It requires the ability to tune into nature and the desire to be a benign presence within nature and society.

EAT

glitter

FOR
BREAKFAST
AND SHINE
ALL DAY

WHERE ARE YOU NOW? INSIDE? READING THIS ON A SCREEN? ON A TRAIN?

The first and most important step to living a more magical life is to experience nature in all its vivid glory. Unicorns do not live in offices or apartments, or commute to work in hot metal boxes. No, unicorns live in clouds and woodland glades. So be like the unicorn and get your hooves dirty. Head to the countryside and breathe the fresh air, watch the light change and snort the scent of the forest.

Challenge one

By next month can you find your nearest:

Forest

Lake

Woodland glade

Stream

Wildflower meadow

Challenge two

By next month can you lie down on the ground and enjoy:

One sunset

One dark starry sky

One sunrise

One misty morning

Challenge three

By next month can you spend an hour watching:

A spider weave a web

A bee collect pollen

A stream babbling over stones

The kingdom of mini-beasts on a lawn

Birds flying high above you

NATURE IS A PETRIFIED MAGIC CITY.

NOVALIS

Being in tune with the natural magic all around you is the first trot to being a magical unicorn. The second leap requires the acquisition of gentle emotional intelligence.

Unicorns do not make an enormous song and dance about their magical water purifying abilities. Oh no. They work their magic with the water and then slip away quietly.

So you, too, can follow the unicorn and decide to complete a magical act every day. No one but the unicorn needs to know what you're up to. Think of yourself as the magical unicorn fairy.

Magical unicorns

1. Help people with heavy bags of shopping.

2. Make food parcels for those living alone.

3. Always smile.

4. Befriend the lonely.

5. Give flowers to friends for no reason at all.

6. Notice when someone is upset and make them a cup of tea.

7. Call the person you've been meaning to.

8. Carry out random acts of kindness.

9. Allot real face-to-face time with the people you love.

10. Don't need praise.

I BELIEVE IN
UNICORNS

BE MORE...
FABULOUS

To live
like a
unicorn is
to inhabit
a fabulous
legend.

UNICORNS ARE...
FABULOUS

fæbjʊləs: almost unbelievable, astounding, legendary

Is there a more remarkable creature than the unicorn? Don't be silly darling! The unicorn is the most incredible of fabulous creatures, and can make your life amazing, too. Channel the iridescent horn, the shiny coat and the glossy mane of a unicorn and enter into a world of glittery fabulousness.

It's the horn isn't it? Come on! Have you ever seen such a splendid appendage? It's simply fabulous and the accessory that everybody is talking about.

The other animals are getting ready for a night out. The griffon is fluffing its feathers, the phoenix is blowing out the flames and the dear old dragon is polishing his claws, when the unicorn glides into the glade.

"OMG darling – that horn – it's fabulous."

"Which designer sent it to you?"

"It's so pearly white, spirally and pointy and perfect."

The unicorn simply turns her head gently and continues walking. All that remains is a fabulous shimmer of unicorn shadow.

In 1607, Edward Topsell, the niche blogger of his day, wrote a bestiary, where he recorded seeing King Charles I's unicorn's horn:

"I never saw anything in any creature more worth of praise than this horn. The substance is made by nature, not art, wherein all the markes are fond which the true horn requireth... It is of so great a length that the tallest man can scarcely touch the top thereof, for it doth fully equal seven feet."

And if the horn is not fabulous enough, the Qilin, the Chinese version of the unicorn, is often depicted covered entirely in jewels, stars and gemstones. Part dragon, part deer, part unicorn, the Qilin, has a voice that sounds like the tinkling of bells, or wind chimes, or indeed the wind itself.

"Well, now that we have seen each other," said the Unicorn, "If you'll believe in me, I'll believe in you. Is that a bargain?"
Alice's Adventures Through the Looking Glass, Lewis Carroll

However, it's not simply the divine horn that makes a unicorn fabulous. As all clever unicorns know, looks are not everything.

Take a quick gallop through literature and you'll find the unicorn making legendary appearances, including the Bible, Shakespeare's plays, *Alice Through the Looking Glass*, *The Chronicles of Narnia* and *Harry Potter*.

DISCOVER HOW TO LEAD A LEGENDARY LIFE.

How to find your physical fabulous:

1. Ask your friends which is your finest feature.

2. Believe them.

3. Focus on this one astounding aspect and customize it.

4. Curate this feature so it emerges as your signature look.

5. Rock it daily and with pride (for without her horn, the unicorn's simply a plain old nag).

To be truly
fabulous is
to live a life
that inspires
other great
minds.

Get the fabulous unicorn look:

- Wear more sequins
- Be bold
- Be brave
- Be bright
- Run wild
- Dye your hair
- Be fun
- Be OTT
- Command attention
- Dazzle

Just as the horn makes the unicorn fabulous, there is a sparkly something within each of us that's unique and astounding.

Being truly fabulous is not simply looking majestic; it's living life well and for the good of yourself and others.

Find your equivalent of the unicorn's horn and nurture your own unique talent to become a genuinely fabulous unicorn.

How to find your inner fabulous:

1. What are you fabulous at that no one else is? (Nothing is not an answer!)

2. If you need a nudge remembering, recall what your teachers / colleagues / parents praised in you. Seriously – there will be something.

3. Great – now you've got it. Don't be embarrassed! Whatever your own unique talent is – own it.

4. Plan how to utilize your talent at work, in your social life, for the benefit of others.

5. Work at it. Sure it may be a bit rusty, but buff it up and watch yourself blossom into the mane attraction.

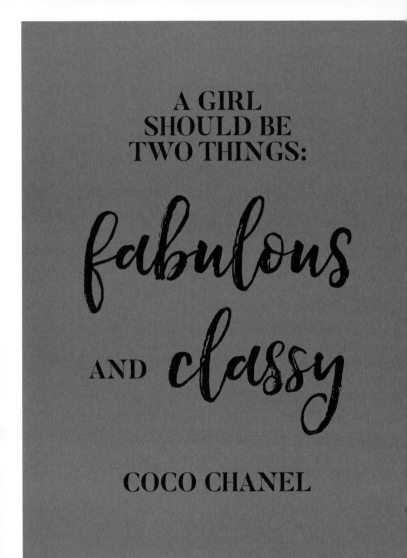

A GIRL
SHOULD BE
TWO THINGS:

fabulous

AND *classy*

COCO CHANEL

To be truly fabulous inside and out:

 Live life at a gallop

 Be kind

Give energy

Love with a passion

 See the fabulous in others

 Be brilliant at something

Keep trying

 Forgive

Be exuberant

Don't bray

BE MORE...
ENIGMATIC

UNICORNS
LIVE IN
WHISPERS
AND DANCE
IN OUR
HEARTS.

UNICORNS ARE...
ENIGMATIC

enɪɡˈmætɪk: difficult to interpret
or understand; mysterious

Behind the glitter and sparkle of the glorious
unicorns we know and love, there lives a
shy, mysterious creature. Tiptoe in to the
woodland glade to discover another side to
the unicorn, a side of shadows and secrets.

Unicorns, those paler than white, single-horned
horses that inhabit our deepest fantasies, walk
softly through the pages of human
history. Some blessed folk have
been lucky enough to witness their
fleeting appearance: a swoosh of
a tail, the flick of a mane. Their
presence whispers at the
edges of our imaginations.

Aristotle, the greatest of all ancient Greek philosophers, believed in their existence, Julius Caesar thought they could be found deep in the darkest of forests, while the earliest recorded sighting is recorded by Ctesias of Cnidus who, in 398 BC, wrote about unicorns in India.

"Their bodies are white, their head dark red and their eyes are dark blue. They have a horn on the forehead, which is about a foot and a half in length. The base of this horn... is pure white; the upper part is sharp and of a vivid crimson; and the remainder, or middle portion, is black."

The unicorn, "likes lonely grazing grounds whereit roams in solitude" Aelian, Roman writer, 3rd century

Picture the scene: a damp woodland, branches creaking underfoot, sunlight peeking through the canopy, and suddenly you see it.

The unicorn. Shimmering in the glade. Through millennia, all have looked and only a few have seen. Those who glimpsed the unicorn through the heavy forest leaves sought to capture the elusive beast in words, pictures and in poetry. And yet, only figments remain. A sighting here, a hope there. The unicorn is forever enigmatic: a mystery of our own making.

Its very enigma is what makes a unicorn so compelling. Does it really exist? Where does it live? Can a unicorn ever be captured? Let the intoxicating allure of enigma work its magic on you. Imagine provoking such enticing questions: Who's that girl? Does anyone really know her? Can she ever be captured?

"There is no beauty without some strangeness"
Edgar Allen Poe

Enigma has spun a wisp of smoke around history's most captivating women — Helen of Troy, Scheherazade, the women behind Bitcoin — to conjure up a select handful. So what if you're not an ancient Greek princess, the storyteller in 1001 Arabian Nights, a reclusive financial genius, or even a unicorn for that matter – you can still draw on the power of enigma to create an aura of mystery around you.

DISCOVER HOW TO SHROUD YOURSELF IN MYSTERY AND ENIGMA.

Don't expose all of yourself:

- Be elusive
  say no to some invitations

- Be unfathomable
  don't explain yourself

- Be puzzling
  ask stimulating questions then disappear

BE ANYTHING BUT

predictable

HOW TO REVEAL LESS

Learn the art of disappearing:

1. Trot away from social media.

2. Don't live through your online feeds.

3. Can you reduce your apps from many to one or two? Or none?

4. Write letters instead of Snapchatting.

5. Draw pictures instead of taking them.

Talk your way to becoming enigmatic:

Cultivate your conversation to stimulate an aura of mystery and excitement.

Don't be afraid to ask wild questions without knowing the answer.

Be prepared to remain silent when you have nothing to say.

Leave halfway through an event.

Never explain where you're going.

Questions enigmatic unicorns ask:

Why do you think that?

Tell me who you are really?

Who do you think I am?

Can you guess my secret?

What's my magical power?

Why be enigmatic?

Awe and speculation is just so smokin' exciting

Mysteries stir powerful emotions

Because everyone loves the hunt

Your unpredictability will dazzle others

Intrigue is the stuff of legends

I AM

power

—

I AM

unicorn

UNICORNS ARE...
POWERFUL

pavǝrfl: having great power or strength

Famous for being impossible to capture, the unicorn is no mere fluffy pony. Its horn is invincible and its flanks are strong. Learn how this most mighty of beasts commands power for good not ill.

From ancient times to the moment you are reading this, unicorns have infused history with power. Neither prancing ponies, nor skittish colts, unicorns are powerful creatures who gallop majestically through our imaginations. Just think of that glorious muscular stallion who leaps through your dreams. From the earliest sightings, unicorns' power has attracted naturalists and historians who have marvelled at their sleek muscles and spirited instincts.

"The creature has the most discordant and powerful voice of all animals. When other animals approach, it does not object but is gentle with its own kind, however it is inclined to be quarrelsome." Aelian, Roman writer, 3rd century

With unicorns, their protective instinct is key. They will not desert their offspring, nor harm the weak. For true power is the ability to deploy it kindly – for the protection and good of others.

Ancient sources report that the powerful unicorn would rather fight to the death than be taken alive, while Jewish tradition tells that the unicorn will never be captured.

"The only way to capture unicorns: when they take their young to pasture you must surround them with many men and horses. They will not desert their offspring and fight with horn, teeth and heels; and they kill many horses and men... They cannot be caught alive." Ctesias of Cnidus, ancient Greek physician, 5th century BC

To harness the power of the unicorn is to harness your own majestic creature within. Clasp its muscular back, clutch your legs around its flanks, lean into its firm neck and ride your inner unicorn as powerfully as you dare.

"Most powerful is he who has himself in his own power." Seneca, Roman author

NOTHING IS
MORE POWERFUL
THAN A WOMAN
WHOSE TIME
HAS COME.

HOW TO BE PHYSICALLY POWERFUL

Physical strength comes naturally to the unicorn but sometimes it needs to be honed in humans (yes the all-seeing unicorn has its eye on you sleepyhead). We're not thinking body builders here, though they are certainly welcome. Your muscles needn't necessarily bulge but they ought to be put through their paces. Whatever your physical preference, be it anything from netball and yoga to ballet and rugby, do it well and with gusto.

To make the most of your physical power:

- ● **Eat well**
- ● **Exercise well**
- ● **Sleep well**

These three tiny gems of wisdom are really important – don't ignore them!

So, the inner power is there in all its unicorn glory. Now, to the really tricky part: how to exude power? It's easy for the unicorn – being white with a massive horn – it really ought to check its privilege. But we'll let it off. To be powerful is not only to know your own strength but to reveal it to others as well.

Here are five tips that, if adopted, instantly make the user a conductor of the most lightning form of power.

Powerful unicorns:

1. Always look people in the eye

2. Always dress smartly

3. Always control their temper

4. Always work out their own problems

5. Always distinguish themselves

"YOU HAVE POWER OVER YOUR MIND. NOT OUTSIDE EVENTS. REALISE THIS AND YOU WILL FIND STRENGTH."

MARCUS AURELIUS,
ROMAN EMPEROR

HOW TO FIND OUT WHAT MAKES YOU FEEL POWERFUL.

On a dark winter's afternoon when your hot chocolate is skimming over, your onesie needs an extra blanket and you might just have one more biscuit... On that day, it can be hard to feel powerful. In those instances it's important to be able to access the prompt that revs you up again, that puts the air beneath your wings and will make you bolt like the unicorn.

Exercise one:

That feeling. The one where you can conquer the world. It's the feeling in the pit of your stomach. It's the gallop in your step, the swagger in your haunches and the toss of your mane. Yes that one. It is power. What causes it? Let's find out.

1. On a blank piece of paper write in capital letters: THESE MAKE ME FEEL AS POWERFUL AS A UNICORN

2. Beneath, write down your favourite:

Song	Image	Idol
Exercise	Food	Ability
Shoe	Outfit	Accessory
Friend	Relative	View

3. Place the paper somewhere safe.

4. Next time you need to harness your inner strength, choose one item from the list and do it. Enjoy it. Eat it. Wear it. Phone it. See it. Do it.

5. Be powerful.

THE
MEASURE OF
A PERSON IS
WHAT THEY
DO WITH
POWER.

To be truly powerful is to use your power to great effect. The unicorn uses its power to defend its young, weaker creatures and themselves from harm. Unicorns do not use power for their own sake. Therefore, be like the unicorn and use your power for the good of others.

Remember, those with power must, like the unicorn, use it gently. To be a powerful unicorn:

★ **Defend truth**

★ **Defend justice**

★ **Defend children**

★ **Defend animals**

★ **Defend yourself**

BE MORE...
GRACEFUL

Breathe like
a unicorn,
live like
a unicorn,
love like
a unicorn.

UNICORNS ARE... GRACEFUL

'greɪsfl: having or showing grace or elegance

With its equine grace and elegant horn, the unicorn glides effortlessly through history. Let the poise of the unicorn add charm and sophistication to life in the real world today.

When light was new and the world was stretching awake, Adam named the animals... so the story goes. Those that crawled and crept, came to him, and those that flew, swept down from the sky. Adam decided to name the unicorn first. As he did so, God reached down and touched the unicorn's single horn. Ever afterwards, the unicorn was elevated above all other animals.

The unicorn walks amidst our fables and stories with a grace unlike any other creature. From the unicorn in sumptuous medieval tapestries to the unicorn in *Harry Potter*, this elegant equine has encapsulated an ethereal elegance.

"Grace is beauty that never fades."

We all know the creature. She has a silken mane and walks with her perfectly structured nose in the air. She glides through rooms, her behind swaying gently. And then she turns and looks at you. And smiles. And you melt, as she has kindness in her eyes.

She is the unicorn and she is graceful. Unicorns are not mere show ponies. They have an inner grace and dignity that distinguishes them from other beasts of the field. Likewise, harness the unicorn's grace and you too can elevate yourself from the herd.

"The unicorn likes lonely grazing grounds where it roams in solitude." Aelian, Roman writer, 3rd century

Yes, we all know that we should "be ourselves" but really, we can all learn a little from the goddess that is the unicorn. She doesn't keep her coat that white, her horn that shimmery and her poise that perfect without a teeny bit of effort. You wouldn't find the unicorn slouching over her iPhone or eating with her mouth open. Oh no. True unicorns are graceful inside and out.

HOW TO LOOK GRACEFUL
IN FIVE EASY WAYS:

1. Perfect your posture – walk with shoulders back, chin forward and with purpose.

2. Eat nicely – mouth closed, chewing slowly, wiping if necessary, no phones at the manger.

3. Care for the small details – fingernails, eyelashes and hooves.

4. Dress elegantly – sure the unicorn's naked, but she doesn't flaunt her intimate parts.

5. Tend your mane – all graceful unicorns need gorgeous hair.

I DON'T SWEAT,
I SPARKLE

How to be graceful on the inside:

1. Be kind: less bitter more glitter

2. Be caring: dare to care

3. Be forgiving: move on, be strong

4. Be magnanimous: in victory, grace

5. Be polite: more clout, don't shout

TEST YOURSELF: CAN YOU BE A GRACEFUL UNICORN?

Can you?

1. Walk across the room with a book on your head?

2. Flick your mane and walk away when some old nag is mean to you?

3. Spend a whole day without swearing?

4. Be charming to everyone you speak to?

5. Always remember to say please and thank you?

6. Eat *clam vongole* without dribbling?

7. Open the door for whoever crosses your path?

8. Listen to whoever is speaking to you?

9. Not get drunk?

10. Cross your legs at the ankle not the knee?

BE MORE...
CHIMERA

UNICORNS ARE A CRAZY MISHMASH OF OUR FAR-OUT FANTASIES.

UNICORNS ARE...
CHIMERA

kaɪ'mɪərə: an imaginary creature compounded of incongruous parts; an impossible idea or hope

In art and folklore, not all unicorns are white horses with horns. Sometimes they are small, like lapdogs, and other times as large as elephants. Remember, you don't have to be perfect to be a unicorn.

So that cute white unicorn you're picturing now, with its bright white flanks and pearlescent horn, may not be an entirely accurate rendition. Let's be honest here, unicorns are not My Little Ponies for grown-ups. Over the centuries, unicorns have appeared goat-like, lion-like, dog-like and even a mixture of all three. If humans have been myth-making about the unicorn for over 4,000 years, chances are the creature will have morphed wildly in both form and function.

Leonardo Da Vinci drew the unicorn with a horse's body, a goat's feet and a lion's mane.

"The unicorn is a very small animal like a kid excessively swift." Physiologus, Ancient Greek bestiary

Raphael painted the unicorn as small as a lapdog cradled carefully in a young woman's skirts. *The Spiderwick Chronicles* feature unicorns with deer-like bodies, shaggy manes and tails ending in a puff of fur.

"They have the hair of a buffalo and feet like an elephant's. They have a single large black horn in the middle of the forehead... They have a head like a wild boar's... They spend their time by preference wallowing in mud and slime. They are very ugly brutes to look at. They are not at all such as we describe them." Marco Polo, 13th century adventurer

If unicorns don't fit the mould – why should you?

Much of the glorious charm of the unicorn lies in its very melding of assorted creatures. Whether goat-like, deer-like, or lion-like, the unicorn with its gleaming horn and mystical pull does not need to be a perfectly white horse to be faultless.

And nor do you. If your mane is sleek but your feet are too goat-like for comfort, fear not, you're in good company. Who wants to be conventional anyway?

Just as the unicorn has been moulded by those genius storytellers and artists through the ages, so, too, are you the result of generations of shifting form – the nose of your great-grandmother, the ears of your great-great uncle, the twinkle in the eye of your mother.

"The whole is more than the sum of its parts." Aristotle

EMBRACE YOUR INCONGRUOUS PARTS

 Don't conform

Don't seek to join the herd

Don't hide

Do be absurd

Do clash

Do change

HOW TO CHERISH YOUR DIFFERENT PARTS

Try this exercise:

1. Look in the mirror holding only a pen and paper.

2. Look at your hair. Is it more like your mother or father's or one of your grandparents'?

3. Now look at your face. Are the ears really your own? Your nose? Your mouth?

4. Where in your fabulous mixed heritage have your features come from?

5. Work your way down from your chin to your toes, noting down the gifts from the past that is your current body.

6. Write "thank you" next to each observation.

Now try this:

1. Look in the mirror holding only a pen and paper.

2. Look at your face and body and note down what is truly your own.

3. Write "thank you" next to each observation.

Never forget... goat's feet, big cat fur and rhino hide have all variously melded together to form the exquisite unicorn. So, too, have your different body parts been melded together, whether you love or loathe them, to make you – the exquisite you reflected in the mirror.

Even with a hind as wide as a rhino's and hooves as gnarled as a hog's, unicorns are still the most awesome creature around. They're unicorns, whether perfectly pretty or muddily ugly, they're unicorns and they're proud. The same should go for you. Once you've embraced all your strange body parts, be like the chimera unicorn and wear your peculiarities with pride.

**MAKE THE
MOST OF THE**

BEST

**AND THE
LEAST OF THE**

WORST

Five golden rules for all those exotic-looking unicorns out there:

1. Accept how you look. Confidence is key for all creatures.

2. Make the most of your strangest parts. Dress to suit your greyhound legs or rhino skin.

3. Let your personality trump your looks, no matter how splendid.

4. Play the hand you're dealt with.

5. Smile more.

BE MORE...
PLAYFUL

**UNICORNS PLAY
FOREVER IN OUR**

imagination

UNICORNS ARE...
PLAYFUL

ˈpleɪfʊl: full of fun; wanting to play

What could be more fun than hanging out with unicorns on a bed of blossom or high up on a rainbow? Being playful isn't just for children and unicorns – climb aboard the rainbow and join the party.

Splosh, splat and then down with a thunderous wet; the rains start to fall. The echoes of the final hammering resound in the valley. Noah and his family summon the animals two by two – crocodiles, peacocks, beetles, giraffes, flamingos; the whole caboodle. They ascend the wooden ark to shelter from the deluge. Noah is about to board up the entrance when he spies the final pair oblivious on a distant hillside.

"Come unicorns," he beckons.

But they are too busy playing
to pay him any attention. They
dance in the rain; they shake their
manes at each other and toy with their
hooves in the pouring air.

"Come unicorns," Noah tries again, shouting
through the bucketing skies.

As the water rises to their ankles they canter
about happier than ever. It rises to their knees
and still they play. They are too busy laughing with
each other to notice that the ship is sailing.

"Come unicorns," Noah shouts one last time as
the ark bobs up and down on the water.

"Why, this is fun!", they shriek as the water rises to
their knees, then their shoulders. What's this? They
find themselves swimming, and still they laugh,
their bubbles of giggles rising with the flood.

Even in a disaster, as all encompassing as Noah's flood, the unicorn still manages to triumph. Too busy playing to board the ark, it doesn't mean that the unicorns became forever extinct. Legend tells us that as the waters rose around their silky white coats, the unicorns embraced the waves and they began swimming.

The unicorns survived the deluge by continuing to play underwater. They kicked and splashed their way through the watery flood until eventually they didn't need their legs any more. Their silvery tail hardened and their front legs became fins. Their horns continued to grow and they ploughed their way through the icy deep.

After hundreds of years the unicorns transformed into the narwhal, a beautiful arctic whale with a two-metre (seven-foot) long tusk. Narwhals*, known as unicorns of the sea, still elicit mysterious awe when spied by sailors today.

*So majestic are these creatures that the Throne Chair of Denmark is made of Narwhal tusks.

Playfulness is what makes us **human**. Doing pointless, purposeless things, just for **fun**.

Matthew Parris,
journalist

You are a rare and beautiful creature, full of wonder – let us play together.

Be like the playful unicorn and keep finding joy in life, even when it starts raining. Sometimes events will swamp you and you'll feel as if you're drowning, but... continue frolicking. And if you go under... keep swimming and transform yourself into something equally enthralling.

BE MORE PLAYFUL UNICORN

Discover how to live a playful life

Reconnect with the child within:

1. Keep a picture of yourself as a child on display.

2. Write down your three favourite childhood games, then play them.

3. Tickle a friend.

Access your inner creativity:

1. Share your skills with others. If you're good at dancing, teach a non-dancer to dance.

2. Dance, sing, paint – alone if needs be.

3. Now dance, sing and paint with friends.

Be open to spontaneity:

1. Say yes.

2. When the buzz creeps up on you, clasp it and run with it.

3. Try something new every day.

WE DON'T
STOP PLAYING
BECAUSE WE
GROW OLD;
WE GROW OLD
BECAUSE WE
STOP PLAYING.

GEORGE BERNARD SHAW

10 SURE-FIRE PLAYFUL ACTIVITIES

1. Play catch the egg (shell on, but uncooked of course).

2. Water fight!

3. Play with a kitten.

4. Make a model out of balloons and squirty cream.

5. Food fight!

6. Play twister.

7. Have a mouths–only jelly eating competition.

8. Play with a puppy.

9. Blindfold yourself and a friend and feed each other.

10. Bubble wrap disco.

BE MORE...
FIERCE

Don't *fence* me in.

UNICORNS ARE...
FIERCE

fɪəs: angry or aggressive in a way that is frightening

Unicorns are not pets. They have never been domesticated and fight ferociously with their horns. Discover why looking hot is not a barrier to being fierce.

As splendid as it is, that horn is not simply worn by the unicorn to look sassy. Oh no. That horn is a symbol of power, of strength, of ferocity.

From ancient times unicorns have been recognized as fierce creatures whose horn embodies invincible strength.

"People say he is completely invincible and that his whole strength lies in his horn. When he knows he is being pursued by many hunters and about to be captured, he leaps up to a cliff top and throws himself down from it, and as he falls he turns himself in such a way that his horn completely cushions the shock and he escapes unharmed." Cosmas Indicopleustes, a Greek traveller from Alexandria in Egypt in 6th century

When later adventurers roamed the world in search of the unicorn, reports trickled in of a wild herd of single-horned horses who lived fierce lives on the plains of Tibet. They were almost impossible to catch and fought with a ferocity that both provoked alarm and admiration.

"A native of the interior of Tibet, fierce and extremely wild, seldom, if ever, caught alive. They go together in herds."

Major Latter in a letter about unicorns published in the 1821 Quarterly Journal.

In medieval heraldry, when a fierce creature brave enough to take on the English lion was needed, the unicorn was deemed perfect to represent Scotland. From the 12th century onwards it has been rearing upright, fighting, with the crown about its neck.

The lion and unicorn are to this day symbols of the United Kingdom and make up part of the Royal Coat of Arms. You'll spot the unicorn everywhere now, fighting the lion on shields, on plaques – even on British pound coins.

And now... book your ticket to Scotland because the unicorn is still the national animal of Scotland. It's so much cooler than Japan's carp, for instance. Just saying...

Sometimes, it's not enough to be beautiful and strong. Sometimes a little fire is needed, a little vigour, a little verve. And sometimes, a huge, massive, gigantic bellow of animal intensity is required. There's no need for violence, but there is a need to tap into the invincibility of the unicorn's horn.

Fierce unicorns are strong, tenacious, courageous, loyal, motivated, honest and independent. And they will not be hemmed in by society's demands of them. One of the most potent elements of unicorn mythology is their wildness – no one keeps a unicorn as a pet. A fierce unicorn is still innocent, it's still graceful and it's still magical. It's not fierce unless absolutely necessary. It does not provoke, it just defends.

WHEN TO BE FIERCE?

Exercise one:

Tick any of the statements
below you recognize:

- I've felt uncomfortable.

- I've witnessed an unpleasant act.

- The news has made me feel sad.

- A loved one has been upset.

- You've wanted to escape a situation.

If you've ticked at least one, you've identified a time to be fierce. Being fierce can help:

※ **Stop injustice**

※ **Stop unkindness**

※ **Stop harm**

How to be fierce?

1. Trust your instincts

2. Be brave

3. Learn to speak with a loud, confident voice

4. Be firm

5. Maintain eye contact

6. Be prepared to wait

HOW TO BE PRACTICALLY FIERCE

True ferocity is not simply a blind flash of anger deployed occasionally. It's passion for a cause – it is fighting the good fight.

To be long-term fierce consider:

1. Joining a political party.

2. Volunteering for a charity.

3. Writing letters / blogs or making vlogs about your chosen cause.

4. Hanging out with other fierce unicorns who share your passion.

Exercise two:

If being fierce doesn't come naturally, spend some time in the mirror practising. Try saying these out loud:

1. No thanks.

2. Not on my watch.

3. No way.

4. I disagree.

5. Not for me.

6. Stop right there.

7. This is wrong.

8. I will do as I please.

9. I can't take this on now.

10. I am unicorn.

THOUGH SHE BE BUT LITTLE,

she is

fierce

SHAKESPEARE

BE MORE...
INNOCENT

TRUE INNOCENCE IS AS PRECIOUS AS A UNICORN FOAL

UNICORNS ARE... INNOCENT

ˈɪnəsnt: a pure, guileless person

The innocence of the unicorn is one of its most endearing qualities. Forget ambition, forget cynicism, forget mockery and remember what it's like to be an innocent creature in a beautiful world.

Are you ready? Things are going to get pretty cute around about now. Sit tight and prepare to coo because we're going to pad gently over to unicorn foals. Yes, the most innocent creatures in the woodland glade.

When you read this, make sure you whisper because you won't want to wake them...

Some storytellers say unicorn foals are born pure gold. They turn silver at two and have a hide so white it makes the snow look grey.

Others write that unicorn foals are born in the heart of a blossom. On the first ray of spring sunshine, the petals open and out trots a staggering baby unicorn. It steps gently down onto the leaves and branches, but floats the final jump to the woodland floor.

Too pure to be born on earth, others write that unicorn foals emerge perfectly formed from clouds. They glide gently towards earth bringing with them the silver shimmer of heaven.

INNOCENCE IS LIKE POLISHED ARMOUR; IT

adorns AND *defends*

ROBERT SOUTH, POET

Conjured into existence for its sheer beauty, the unicorn is the only mythical creature not fashioned out of human fears.

Usually when legends appear they speak to the darkest of nightmares. Think of those terrifying monsters that slept under your bed. Remember the child-eating witches of fairy tales. Dare to look at the monsters that sweep through our blackest visions – werewolves, sea serpents, vampires – all vile creatures. Not so the unicorn. We do not fear it. It does not frighten us. It is simply wonderful.

It does no harm.
It does not terrify.
It does not frighten.
It is as innocent as the lamb.

As if that wasn't cotton-tail innocent enough, the Qilin, the unicorn of Eastern tradition, is reputed to be so gentle that it will not eat flesh and walks so softly that it will not harm even a blade of grass.

The wistful innocence of the unicorn has spawned some of the most magnificent medieval art ever created. In the 15th century medieval Europe was entranced by the legend of the innocent unicorn and vast tapestries were spun in wool, silk, silver and gold thread. Hanging in fairytale castles and bought in later centuries by museums for vast sums, the unicorn tapestries all focused particularly on one element of the unicorn: its innocence.

It is recorded by many that the only way to capture a unicorn was to send a young virgin girl into the forest. She would tiptoe into the glade, rest against a tree and soon the unicorn – recognizing a fellow innocent soul – would lie down in the girl's lap.

"The unicorn, through its intemperance and not knowing how to control itself, for the love it bears to fair maidens forgets its ferocity and wildness; and laying aside all fear it will go up to a seated damsel and go to sleep in her lap, and thus the hunters take it." Leonardo da Vinci

HOW TO BE MORE INNOCENT

Sure, it's great to be confident, dramatic and loud, but sometimes among all the various squads of people, there are those background people, the quieter types; the people who like to be left alone. They walk softly amidst the clamour and their innocence deflects attention.

 To be innocent is not to be guillable, nor a doormat, nor a fool.

 To be innocent is to be given freedom to pursue your endeavours.

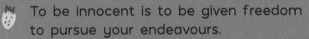 To be innocent is to be respectful of creation and those around you.

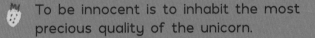 To be innocent is to inhabit the most precious quality of the unicorn.

How to reclaim your innocence:

Only young children are truly innocent, but with a few reminders innocence can be recaptured in later life.

1. Spend time with small children.

2. Spend time with animals.

3. Spend time in nature.

4. Make time for your favourite charitable causes.

5. Make time for those you love.

6. Make time to smile.

Innocence is one of the most exciting things in the world.

Eartha Kitt, singer

How to create the innocent look:

1. Wear natural fabrics: cotton, wool, cashmere and linen.

2. Wipe away the make-up.

3. Slip into ballet shoes rather than stilettos.

4. Swerve away from hair dye.

5. Dab on rose water rather than perfume.

6. Cut, rather than paint your nails.

7. Go for gingham fabrics.

8. Try plaits (braids), bunches and flowers in your hair.

True innocence is a state of mind. It's impossible to be good all the time – no one is trying to create a vanilla unicorn here – but the world could all do with a little more gentleness.

Innocent unicorns...

- Don't seek out ugliness or malice

- Are not crude (sure, there's a myth that unicorns may fart rainbows but they don't boast about it)

- Try not to argue (think of unicorn foals instead)

- Choose optimism over pessimism

- Use their eyes to great effect (just think of those lovely long lashes!)

TRY TO BE A

rainbow

IN SOMEONE'S
CLOUD.

MAYA ANGELOU,
AUTHOR

BE MORE...
FULFILLED

Unleash

YOUR INNER
UNICORN

UNICORNS ARE...
FULFILLED

fʊlˈfɪld: satisfied or happy because of fully developing one's abilities or character

If the unicorn can do it (rock that horn and live a life of rainbow sparkles), then why can't we? We can. Believe in unicorns and reach your potential!

Unicorns are mares with bells on. They are horses with bling. They are stallions with added extras. Unicorns are blissed-out fulfilled ponies. Unicorns have fulfilled their equine potential by a rainbow mile.

Unicorns are the embodiment of human desire. We have dreamed of something gorgeous with a horn, so we have imagined the unicorn into existence. It's not too much of a stretch to put the existence of the unicorn down to positive thinking alone.

If positive thinking through the ages can conjure up a creature as downright crazy cute as the unicorn, imagine what the power of positive thought can do for you.

"Shoot for the moon. Even if you miss it you will land among the stars." Lester Louis Brown, American writer

If unicorns represent the pinnacle of human imagination, then how about putting some of this creativity back to work. Use the sheer glory of the unicorn to unleash your inner unicorn and find deep fulfilment.

Every soul on earth possesses something unique to them. Sometimes the gorgeous unicorn within us gets squashed by outside pressures, such as college, work, society. And yet the unicorn within never entirely disappears. It emits a soft silver glow that can flare into rainbow brilliance with just a little tender loving care. Harness your internal unicorn to reach your full potential.

Unicorns are not content living in paddocks and eating hay. Oh no, that's for the herd. Unicorns live in La La Land, they travel by rainbow and holiday in heaven. Hay? Don't be ridiculous! Unicorns eat nothing but freshly spun whispers, warm love hearts and mouthfuls of dreams.

Be like the fulfilled unicorn and refuse to accept the ordinary.

The future
belongs to
those who
believe in
the beauty
of their

Eleanor Roosevelt

ALL OUR DREAMS CAN COME TRUE IF WE HAVE THE COURAGE TO PURSUE THEM.

WALT DISNEY

FIND YOUR POTENTIAL

Exercise one:

1. Find three sheets of paper and a set of colouring pencils.

2. Draw your ideal living space, your ideal partner and you – working at your ideal job.

3. Don't throw them away! Even if the drawings are a little child-like it will help remind you that dreams are for adults, too.

4. Pin the pictures up.

5. Make a promise to yourself not to take them down until you've fulfilled your visions.

Sure, dreaming is important, but so is sheer hard work. Sadly, there's no getting around it. To fulfil your potential and find fulfilment you'll have to work those little hooves right off. But think how proud you'll make the unicorns waiting up in the clouds for you to join their ranks.

How to fulfill your potential:

1. Decide you're going to fulfil your potential. Today.

2. Set small realistic goals.

3. Up skill: it's never too late for re-education.

4. Beat the herd: start earlier and work later.

5. Never give up.

How to find fulfillment and exceed your potential:

1. Never give up.

2. Think BIG.

3. Leap those fences: break out of your comfort zone.

4. Take risks.

5. Go where the stars take you.

KEEP TRUE TO THE DREAMS OF YOUR YOUTH.

FRIEDRICH SCHILLER,
PLAYWRIGHT

UNICORN GLOSSARY

Alicorn: the horn of a unicorn (in reality the horn of a narwhal but don't tell anyone).

#awesomeunicorn: as awesome as unicorns are awesome. That's pretty awesome.

#basicallyaunicorn: one of those magical days when life is so amazing you may as well be a unicorn.

Blossom: flowery explanation for where unicorn foals are born. Always pink.

#borntobeaunicorn: forever unique, forever gorgeous, forever a unicorn.

Clouds: another floaty explanation for where unicorn foals are born. Always fluffy.

#Crazyunicornlady: Yes. And?

Flanks: the sides of the unicorn (between the ribs and hips) – perfect for straddling and riding through the woodland glade.

Glitter: the sparkle unicorns create instead of a shadow.

Harry Potter: Voldemort suckled on the blood of a unicorn. Now that is low.

Heraldry: the unicorn graces the coats of arms of Britain and is the national animal of Scotland.

Hoof: whether cloven or uncloven, the unicorn's hoof is edged with silver. Unicorns present the perfect pedicure.

#Iamunicorn: I am special, unicorns are special, therefore I am unicorn. Obvious.

#Ibelieveinunicorns: Don't even think about crushing my dreams.

Mane: Spun silver and gold. Unicorns wash their manes in moonlight and dry them the breath of fairies.

Mythical: The slur that unicorns only exist in myth (see Heraldry / Harry Potter / Twitter).

Narwal: The bubbly unicorn of the sea.

Qilin: The bejewelled unicorn of Chinese tradition (a unicorn with jewels – why didn't I already know this?).

Pegasus: Frequently muddled with unicorns. The Pegasus is the flying horse of Greek mythology, while unicorns are the single-horned but wingless horse. Unicorns, being magical, are of course able to fly, but do not need wings to do so.

Pony: A derogatory term applied to unicorns by jealous creatures.

Rainbows: Where unicorns live. Some vulgarians suggest that unicorns fart rainbows. This is a myth; unicorns do not fart. Some murky sources suggest that occasionally they "whisper wind" but this has NOT been verified.

#rainbowunicorn: Live life full of colour.

#rollmeinfairydustandcallmeaunicorn: This is my magical land and I'm happy to be here.

Tail: Spun silver and gold. It flicks from side to side and gently sways but never swats. Sometimes known as angel's hair.

#teamunicorn: I never give up. Can't catch a unicorn, can't keep me down.

Twitter: also Instagram / Snapchat / Pinterest – The digital equivalent of the woodland glade. The online world where unicorns continue to inspire, motivate and bring rainbow joy to millions.

Publishing Director Sarah Lavelle
Creative director Helen Lewis
Editor Harriet Butt
Designer Emily Lapworth
Illustrator Carolyn Suzuki
Production Director Vincent Smith
Production Controller Tom Moore

Published in 2018 by Quadrille,
an imprint of Hardie Grant
Publishing

Quadrille
52–54 Southwark Street
London SE1 1UN
quadrille.com

Cataloguing in Publication Data: a
catalogue record for this book is
available from the British Library.

Text © Quadrille Publishing 2018
Illustration © Carolyn Suzuki 2018
Design © Quadrille 2018

Reprinted in 2018 (four times)
10 9 8 7 6 5

ISBN 978 1 78713 122 4

Printed in China